H

FIELD GUIDE

Abigail Rutherford

Values and Identification

Published by

 krause publications

A subsidiary of F+W Media, Inc.

700 East State Street • Iola, WI 54990-0001
715-445-2214 • 888-457-2873
www.krausebooks.com

Our toll-free number to place an order or obtain
a free catalog is (800) 258-0929.

Library of Congress Control Number: 2009923221
ISBN 13-digit: 978-1-4402-0239-1
ISBN 10-digit: 1-4402-0239-7

Designed by Rachael Knier
Edited by Mark F. Moran

Printed in China

More Warman's Field Guides

Contents

Introduction

At my most recent auction, I watched a woman jump up and down with excitement when she realized she was the highest bidder on a vintage Hermes crocodile handbag. Her excitement was palpable and everyone in the room felt a sense of happiness knowing how much this purchase meant to her.

This moment then reminded me of the first time I fell in love with a handbag. I was strolling through the streets of Florence, Italy, enjoying the sites and scenery when, suddenly, a beautiful leather handbag caught my eye. I knew I had to have the bag, so I ran into the store and asked the saleswoman to show it to me. The handbag's patina, precise construction and ornate clasp were even more perfect than I had anticipated. I placed the bag on my shoulder and turned to look at myself in the mirror. I immediately felt transformed. It had single-handedly revived my style and my spirit.

Thinking back on both of these moments made me wonder, "Why would I and the woman at my auction react so intensely to such a basic purchase?" After all, it was only a handbag. The answer, then, seemed obvious: The handbag is so much more than just a bag!

The handbag is a 20th-century phenomenon, which, according to Caroline Cox, author of *The Handbag: An Illustrated History,* parallels "women's status vis-a-vis men" and is directly related to "the increase in woman's social mobility and independence." Today's handbags are not only a useful way to carry necessary items, but also act as a vital extension of a woman's body and a means of self-expression. Whether the purse is a work of art or utilitarian, it makes an enduring statement about its owner and the time period in which it was designed. Furthermore, the handbag has drastically changed women's lives and reflects women's growing sense of empowerment.

The handbags featured in this guide showcase the expressive nature of these ubiquitous accessories. Featuring everything from timeless classics such as Hermes' Kelly bag to the ostentatious "minuadieres" of the 1980s to Murakami's contemporary art designs for Louis Vuitton, each bag captures a moment in history and provides insight into its owner.

This guide is divided into six sections: Architectural, Evening, Exotic, Iconic, Pop Art/Novelty and Timeless. Each section offers an estimated fair market value range and provides insight into other potential condition issues. I hope the insider tips and information that fill these pages help you better understand the handbag market and help ensure your emotions don't get the best of you during your next auction—although, we all know how difficult that can be!

It's in the bag

There are a few factors that can affect the value of a handbag. First and foremost is general condition. When looking at condition issues, the main question is: How much it has been loved. The better the condition, the higher the value. Look at corners, handles, any beaded fringe, interiors and (with animal skins) check for dryness and cracking. All these will affect the overall price of a handbag.

Another issue to be wary of is counterfeit bags. These are worthless, even if you give the disclaimer that it is a knockoff. A good rule of thumb is, when approaching a "designer" handbag, you should always assume it is not right and let the bag prove to you why it is real. This can generally be seen in the overall appearance of the handbag.

There are a couple of questions to ask yourself: Is this handbag well made? With an investment-grade handbag, craftsmanship is generally flawless. Does the logo look right? It is always best to compare to one you know is right. Has it worn well? If the wear is exposing any sort of cheap and poor craftsmanship, then it is probably a counterfeit because these are meant to last a lifetime. Is everything in the right place with the trademarks and stamps? These all can generally be telltale signs.

The last factor is size. A larger the size does not always mean a higher price. For example, Judith Leiber Minaudieres are much more expensive then her larger lizard-skin bags. On the other hand, with Hermes Birkins and Kellys, the bigger they are, the more they seem to cost. Exotic skins can be held in the same regard. (Note: Dimensions in this book do not include handles.)

Acknowledgements

I would like to acknowledge a few people who helped make this book possible: Leslie Hindman, Zoe Bare, Jessica Rodriguez, Yvonne Lopez, Emily Watt, Andy Meyer, and Wesley Donohoe. I would also like to acknowledge the auction houses that made the extent of this collection possible: Leslie Hindman Auctioneers, Wright, Kerry Taylor, Skinner Inc., Ritchies, Dawson and Nye, Karen Augusta, Rago Arts and Auction Center, and Pook and Pook.

Architectural

Architectural

From Pucci's multicolor prints to Lucite box bags to Pierre Cardin's space age shapes, these bags are "sculpturesque." With their geometric lines and shapes and a multitude of materials, these bags are not only functional, but can also be displayed as if works of art. Each designer approached the handbag in such a way that changed the shape of things to come.

Condition Issues: Lucite can scratch quite easily and tends to fog with age and improper storage. In both instances, this can devalue the piece. If Pucci silks are stained, they may be difficult to clean.

10 *Warman's Handbags Field Guide*

Alligator, mid-20th century, 13" x 8" .... **$300-$500**

Leslie Hindman Auctioneers

Alligator, mid-20th century, 14" x 8" .... **$400-$600**

Leslie Hindman Auctioneers

Art Deco Clutch, early 20th century, 3 1/4" x 5 1/2" .... **$150-$250**

Dawson and Nye Auctioneers

Charles Jourdan, late 20th century, 8" x 5" .... **$50-$100**

Leslie Hindman Auctioneers

Charles Jourdan, late 20th century, 12" x 7" .... **$50-$100**

Leslie Hindman Auctioneers

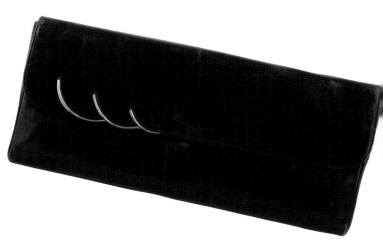

Charles Jourdan, late 20th century, 12" x 6" .... **$50-$100**

Leslie Hindman Auctioneers

Charles S. Kahn, Lucite and faux tortoiseshell box bag, mid-20th century, 3 1/2" x 8" x 4", ... **$275-$325**

Courtesy Stacy LoAlbo

Courreges, late 20th century, 8" x 7" .... **$150-$250**

Leslie Hindman Auctioneers

Courreges, late 20th century, 9" x 6 1/2" .... **$150-$250**

Leslie Hindman Auctioneers

Emilio Pucci, late 20th century, 9 1/2" x 11 1/4"............... **$100-$200**

Leslie Hindman Auctioneers

Emilio Pucci, mid-20th century, 7" x 4" .... **$50-$100**

Leslie Hindman Auctioneers

Emilio Pucci, mid-20th century, 8" x 4 1/2" .... **$100-$200**

Leslie Hindman Auctioneers

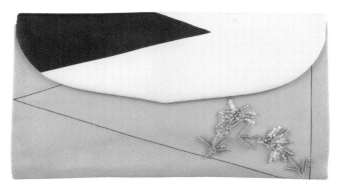

There are a lot of similar Pucci-esque fabrics out there, Emilio Pucci will always have the word Emilio intertwined into the print which can be seen in this close up. Also note beaded detail on reverse.

Emilio Pucci, mid-20th century, 9" x 11" .... **$150-$250**

Kerry Taylor Auctions

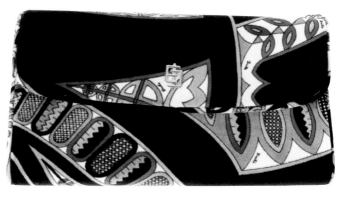

Emilio Pucci, late 20th century, 10" x 6" .... **$200-$300**

Leslie Hindman Auctioneers

Emilio Pucci, late 20th century, 9" x 4 1/2".......................... **$300-$500**

Leslie Hindman Auctioneers

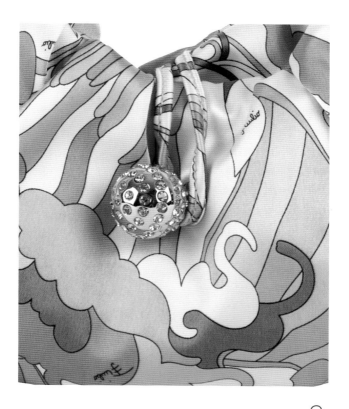

Emilio Pucci, mid-20th century, 5" x 5 1/2".......................... **$400-$600**

Leslie Hindman Auctioneers

Florida Handbags, Lucite, mid-20th century, 7" x 5 1/4" .. **$300-$500**

Wright

Florida Handbags, Lucite, mid-20th century, 7 1/2" x 5" ...... **$300-$500**

Wright

Judith Leiber

Judith Leiber, a Hungarian native, founded her handbag company in 1963. Her now-famous minaudieres originated when she ordered a small metal box as a gift for a friend. When it arrived, Leiber discovered it was badly scratched. She covered the damage with small crystals, and a handbag icon was born.

For half a century, most every First Lady has carried a custom Judith Leiber bag on Inauguration Day.

Judith Leiber, late 20th century, 8 1/2" X 4" x 4" .... **$100-$200**

Leslie Hindman Auctioneers

Koret, Suede, Lucite, mid-20th century, 10 1/2" x 7".......... **$100-$200**

Leslie Hindman Auctioneers

Llewellyn, Lucite, mid-20th century, 8 3/4" x 5" x 1 3/4"... **$100-$200**

Wright

Lucite, Clutch, mid-20th century, 8" x 6 1/2" .... **$50-$100**

Leslie Hindman Auctioneers

Lucite, mid-20th century, 6" x 3 3/4" x 4" .... **$50-$100**

Leslie Hindman Auctioneers

Lucite, mid-20th century, 7" x 6" .... **$50-$100**

Leslie Hindman Auctioneers

Lucite, mid-20th century; Red: 8" x 8";
Clear: 8 1/2" x 4 1/2" .... **$100-$200 each**

Leslie Hindman Auctioneers

Lucite, mid-20th century, 7" x 4" .... **$50-$100**

Leslie Hindman Auctioneers

Lucite, mid-20th century, 8" x 5" .... **S100-$200**

Leslie Hindman Auctioneers

Lucite, Woven Plastic, mid-20th century, 14" x 7" .... **$50-$100**

Leslie Hindman Auctioneers

Mary Frances, late 20th century, 7" x 7" .... **$100-$200**

Pook and Pook Auctioneers

Missoni, late 20th century, 15" x 8" ....**$100-$200**

Leslie Hindman Auctioneers

Nat Lewis, Leather, Lucite, mid-20th century, 13" x 6" ...... **$100-$200**

Leslie Hindman Auctioneers

Patricia of Miami, Lucite, mid-20th century, 7 3/4" x 3 3/4"...**$200-$400**

Wright

With cover open.

Patricia of Miami, Lucite, mid-20th century, 7 1/2" x 6"... **$200-$400**

Wright

With cover open.

Pierre Cardin, Faux Alligator, late 20th century, 10" x 4"..... **$50-$100**

Leslie Hindman Auctioneers

Pierre Cardin, late 20th century, 8" x 8" .... **$100-$200**

Leslie Hindman Auctioneers

Pierre Cardin, late 20th century, 14 1/2" x 13" .... **$150-$250**

Leslie Hindman Auctioneers

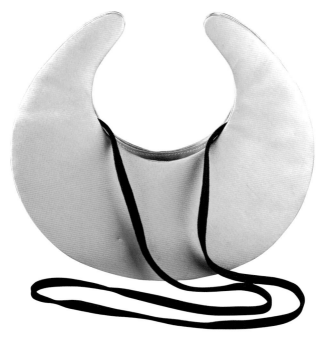

Pierre Cardin, mid-20th century, 10" x 10" .... **$200-$400**

Kerry Taylor Auctions

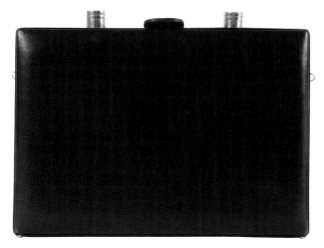

Saks Fifth Avenue, mid-20th century, 8 1/2" x 6 1/4" .... **$100-$200**

Leslie Hindman Auctioneers

Silk, Bakelite; second bag with faux turquoise, early 20th century, each 10" wide...**$75-$150 each**

Ritchies Auctioneers

An easy test for possible Bakelite frames from handbags made in the 1930s, when rubbed to the point of warming, it smells like formaldehyde.

Turtle Skin, Lucite, mid-20th century, 6" x 5"...................... **$50-$100**

Leslie Hindman Auctioneers

Whiting and Davis, Mesh, Lucite, mid-20th century,
13" x 11"... **$200-$400**

Leslie Hindman Auctioneers

Wilardy

Will Hardy joined his family's business, Handbag Specialities of New York, in 1948 and his first inspiration was placing two handles on a jewelry box and looking at it as if it was a handbag. This spawned the idea of using Lucite as a medium (rather than plastic, because it tended to yellow) to create these sculpture-like handbags. His firm, Wilardy Originals, combined his first and last name, and the bags created were first popular in the 1950s. His success was short-lived with the invention of injection molding, the process that could make similar versions at a much cheaper price, and many knockoffs were made, thus diluting the appeal of his bags. Today Wilardy bags are extremely collectible because of their innovative and unusual designs.

Collector Tip: If a handbag appears to have yellowed, while it might be old, it may not be as collectible as Lucite. Also, Lucite tends to fog with age and improper storage, and this will devalue the piece.

Wilardy, Lucite, mid-20th century, 8 1/4" x 6" .... **$600-$800**

Wright

Wilardy, Lucite, mid-20th century, 6 1/4" x 2 1/2" .... **$500-$700**

Wright

Wilardy, Lucite, mid-20th century, 7 1/2" x 4" .... **$600-$800**

Wright

Wilardy, Lucite, mid-20th century, 7 3/4" x 5 1/4" .... **$600-$800**

Wright

Evening

Evening bags are generally the most ornate of any category. From intricate beadwork and all-over crystals to 14k mesh with jeweled clasps, these are often the statement piece for any evening ensemble. This category includes fine creations from the major jewelry houses like Cartier or Tiffany.

Condition Issues: Be aware of loose beading, especially at the fringe, and missing crystals. Since makeup was almost always carried in these bags, be sure to check the interior for staining.

14k Mesh Bag, early 20th century, 5" x 5" ....**$3,000-$5,000**

Leslie Hindman Auctioneers

14k Mesh Bag, mid-20th century, 5" x 7" .... **$2,000-$4,000**

Leslie Hindman Auctioneers

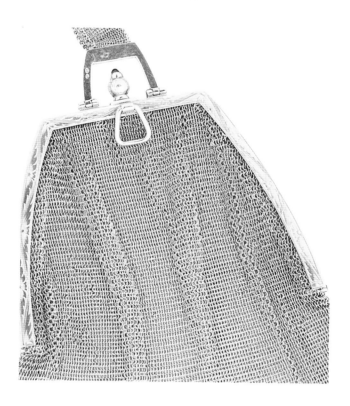

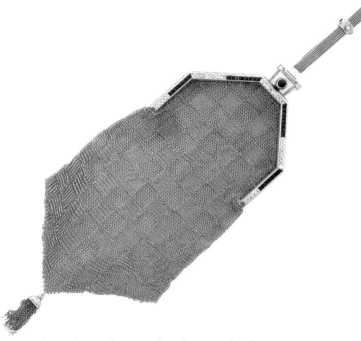

14k Sapphire and Diamond Mesh Bag, mid-20th century,
4" x 8" .... **$2,000-$4,000**

Leslie Hindman Auctioneers

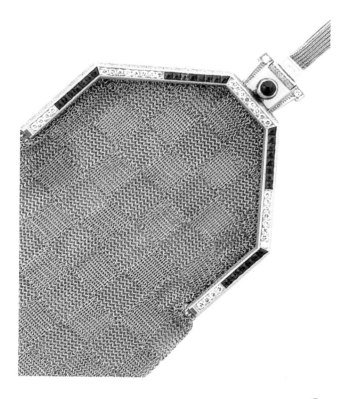

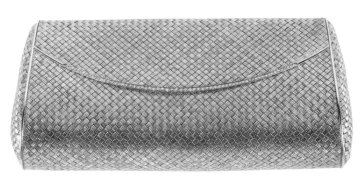

18k Diamond Clutch, mid-20th century, 7" x 3 1/2" .. **$3,000-$5,000**

Leslie Hindman Auctioneers

18k Diamond and Ruby Purse Pendant, mid-20th century, 1 3/4" diameter .... **$1,000-$2,000**

Leslie Hindman Auctioneers

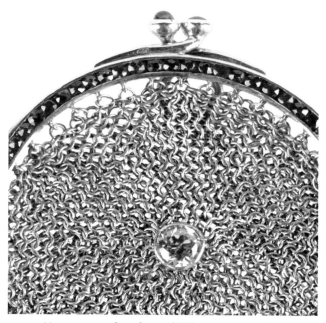

Most common in the early to mid-20th century, evening bags made out of fine gemstones and precious metals were among the truest forms of wealthy extravagance during this period.

Asprey, late 20th century, 9" x 7" .... **$50-$100**

Leslie Hindman Auctioneers

Beaded, early 20th century, 7" x 8" .... **$100-$200**

Leslie Hindman Auctioneers

Beaded, French, mid-20th century, 8" x 7" .... **$50-$100**

Leslie Hindman Auctioneers

Beaded, French, mid-20th century, 8" x 6" .... **$50-$100**

Leslie Hindman Auctioneers

Beaded, French, mid-20th century, 9" x 6" .... **$50-$100**

Leslie Hindman Auctioneers

Beaded, French, mid-20th century, 9" x 6" .... **$50-$100**

Leslie Hindman Auctioneers

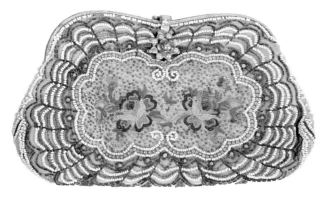

Beaded, French, mid-20th century, 7" x 4" .... **$50-$100**

Leslie Hindman Auctioneers

Beaded, French, mid-20th century, 9" x 5 1/2" .... **$100-$200**

Leslie Hindman Auctioneers

Beaded, French, mid-20th century, 8" x 6" .... **$50-$100**

Leslie Hindman Auctioneers

Beaded, French, mid-20th century, 8" x 6" .... **$50-$100**

Leslie Hindman Auctioneers

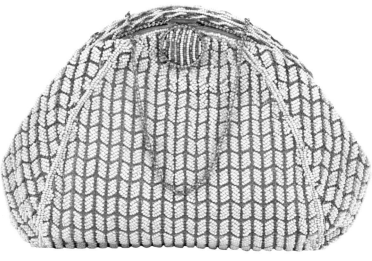

Beaded, French, mid-20th century, 8" x 6" .... **$100-$200**

Leslie Hindman Auctioneers

Beaded, French, mid-20th century, 9" x 5 1/2" .... **$100-$200**

Leslie Hindman Auctioneers

Beaded, French, early 20th century, 7 1/2" x 4".................. **$200-$400**

Leslie Hindman Auctioneers

Among the most collectible forms, French and Belgian beaded bags are acclaimed for the tiny seed-like beads and impeccable craftsmanship that can be seen here.

Beaded, French, mid-20th century, 8 1/2" x 6" .... **$300-$500**

Leslie Hindman Auctioneers

Beaded, French, mid-20th century, 9" x 6 1/2" .... **$300-$500**

Leslie Hindman Auctioneers

Beaded, mid-20th century, 9" x 7" .... **$50-$100**

Leslie Hindman Auctioneers

Beaded, mid-20th century, 7" x 5 1/2" .... **$50-$100**

Leslie Hindman Auctioneers

Beaded, mid-20th century,
6" x 12".............................**$100-$200**

Leslie Hindman Auctioneers

Beaded, mid-20th century,
6" x 12"..................**$100-$200**

Leslie Hindman Auctioneers

Beaded, Swedish, early 20th
century, 3" x 5"... **$100-$200**

Leslie Hindman Auctioneers

Bottega Veneta, Silk, late 20th century, 5" x 9" .... **$50-$100**

Leslie Hindman Auctioneers

Bottega Veneta, Silk, late 20th century, 7" x 10" .... **$300-$500**

Leslie Hindman Auctioneers

Bulgari, late 20th century, 9 1/2" x 8 1/2".......................... **$200-$400**

Leslie Hindman Auctioneers

Cartier, late 20th century, 9" x 8".. **$50-$100**

Leslie Hindman Auctioneers

Cartier, Coral Clasp, mid-20th century, 9 1/2" x 6" ...... **$1,500-$2,500**

Leslie Hindman Auctioneers

Chanel, Velvet, late 20th century, 6 3/4" x 6 1/2".............**$800-$1,200**

Leslie Hindman Auctioneers

Cooper, Beaded, early 20th century, 6" x 6" .... **$50-$100**

Karen Augusta Antique-Fashion

Cooper, Beaded, early 20th century, 8" x 5" .... **$50-$100**

Karen Augusta Antique-Fashion

Elizabeth Arden, mid-20th century, 10" x 5" .... **$100-$200**

Leslie Hindman Auctioneers

Embroidered Evening Bag, Indian, mid-20th century, 8" x 5" . **$300-$500**

Leslie Hindman Auctioneers

Evans, with matching lighter, mid-20th century, 3 1/4" x 5 1/2".. **$50-$100**

Leslie Hindman Auctioneers

Finesse la Model, late 20th century, 6" x 6" .... **$100-$200**

Leslie Hindman Auctioneers

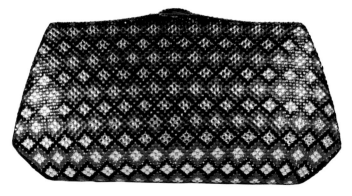

Finesse la Model, late 20th century, 7" x 4" .... **$100-$200**

Leslie Hindman Auctioneers

Hattie Carnegie, mid-20th century, 8" x 10"...................... **$300-$500**

Leslie Hindman Auctioneers

Jacomo, mid-20th century, 7" x 12" .... **$100-$200**

Leslie Hindman Auctioneers

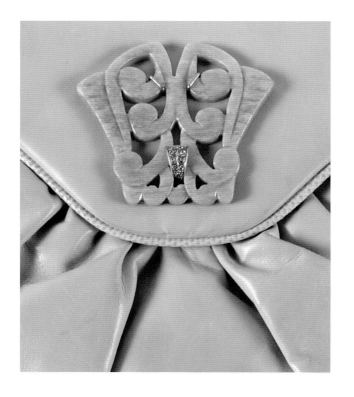

Judith Leiber, late 20th century, 7" x 6" .... **$200-$400**

Leslie Hindman Auctioneers

Judith Leiber, late 20th century, 4" x 3" .... **$400-$600**

Leslie Hindman Auctioneers

Judith Leiber, late 20th century, 6" x 4" .... **$500-$700**

Leslie Hindman Auctioneers

Judith Leiber, late 20th century, 6" x 6 1/2" .... **$800-$1,200**

Leslie Hindman Auctioneers

Judith Leiber, Silk, late 20th century,
5" x 5 1/2" ....**$300-$500**

Leslie Hindman Auctioneers

Judith Leiber, late 20th century, 5" x 8 1/2" .... **$800-$1,200**

Leslie Hindman Auctioneers

Judith Leiber, Suede, late 20th century, 6" x 9" .... **$500-$700**

Leslie Hindman Auctioneers

Kieselstein-Cord, late 20th century, 11" x 5" .... **$300-$500**

Leslie Hindman Auctioneers

Warman's Handbags Field Guide

Mesh Bag, early 20th century,
4" x 5".........................**$50-$100**

Leslie Hindman Auctioneers

Mesh Bag, early 20th century,
  5" x 4 1/2"..........**$50-$100**

Leslie Hindman Auctioneers

Mesh Bag, early 20th century,
4 1/2" x 5"......... **$50-$100**

Leslie Hindman Auctioneers

Mesh Bag, early 20th century, 7 1/2" x 6" .... **$50-$100**

Leslie Hindman Auctioneers

Mesh Bag, early 20th century, 8" x 4" .... **$50-$100**

Leslie Hindman Auctioneers

Paloma Picasso, Book Purse, late 20th century, 5 1/2" x 4" ... **$200-$400**

*Paloma Picasso used a closed book as inspiration
to conceal the items within a handbag.*

Leslie Hindman Auctioneers

Paloma Picasso, Book Purse, late 20th century, 7" x 5 1/2".....**$200-$400**

Leslie Hindman Auctioneers

Nettie Rosenstein, mid-20th century, 9" x 7"..................... **$100-$200**

Leslie Hindman Auctioneers

Petit Point, French, early 20th century............................**$15-$35 each**

Leslie Hindman Auctioneers

Petit Point, French, early 20th century, 8" x 6" .... **$100-$200**

Leslie Hindman Auctioneers

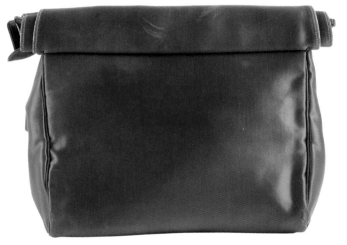

Satin Clutch, early 20th century, 7" x 6" .... **$50-$100**

Leslie Hindman Auctioneers

Satin Clutch, with matching inset, mid-20th century, larger 12" x 6" .... **$50-$100 set**

Leslie Hindman Auctioneers

Satin Clutch, with Marcasite clasp, mid-20th century,
8 3/4" x 5".. **$50-$100**

Leslie Hindman Auctioneers

Sequined, French, mid-20th century, 7 1/2" x 4 3/4"............ **$50-$100**

Leslie Hindman Auctioneers

Silk, early 20th century, 6" x 6"... **$50-$100**

Leslie Hindman Auctioneers

Silk, early 20th century, 5" x 6".. **$50-$100**

Leslie Hindman Auctioneers

Sterling Silver Mesh Bag, early 20th century, 4" x 7".......................... **$200-$400**

Leslie Hindman Auctioneers

Tiffany & Co., Beaded, early 20th century, 5" x 6".......... **$300-$500**

Leslie Hindman Auctioneers

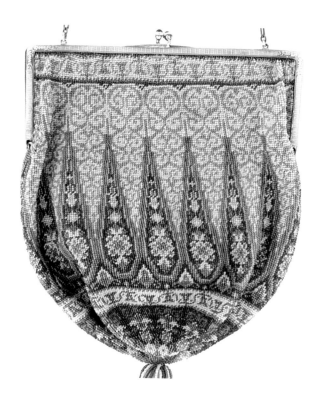

Tiffany & Co., Black Silk, mid-20th century, 7" x 5 1/2"... **$300-$500**

Leslie Hindman Auctioneers

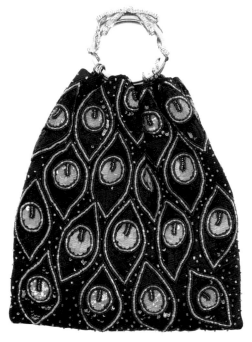

Valentino, Bracelet Bag, late 20th century, 8" x 6 1/2" .... **$200-$400**

Leslie Hindman Auctioneers

Valentino, Bracelet Bag, late 20th century, 10" x 13" .... **$500-$700**

Leslie Hindman Auctioneers

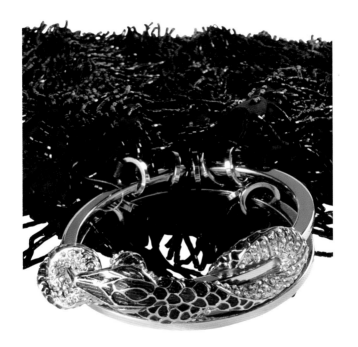

Velvet, early 20th century, 7" x 6" .... **$50-$100**

Leslie Hindman Auctioneers

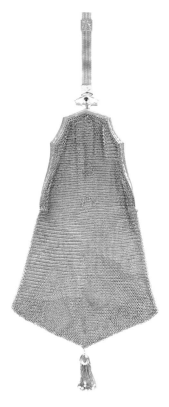

Whiting and Davis, 14k, mid-20th century, 4" x 9" .... **$1,000-$1,500**

Leslie Hindman Auctioneers

Whiting and Davis, 14k,
mid-20th century,
3" x 3"... **$1,000-$1,500**

Leslie Hindman Auctioneers

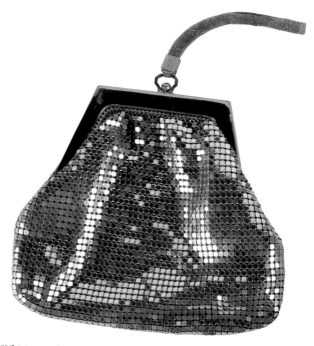

Whiting and Davis, Mesh, mid-20th century, 5 1/4" x 4 1/2". **$25-$50**

Leslie Hindman Auctioneers

Whiting and Davis, Mesh, mid-20th century, 7" x 5" ....**$25-$50**

Leslie Hindman Auctioneers

Whiting and Davis, Mesh, mid-20th century, 5" x 5" .... **$100-$200**

Ritchies Auctioneers

Exotic Skins

Always recognized as the most luxurious of any handbag, these come in all shapes and sizes. While these bags are more expensive because of the hides used, they are generally easy to collect as their strong and durable skin has withstood the test of time. Whether it is an unlabeled classic lizard skin handbag or a rare crocodile Birkin, there are many price points that make this category accessible for almost any collector.

The various exotic skins are highlighted in this section with close-ups to help identify each type.

Condition Issues: Beware of lifting scales and cracking at the handles. The condition of the corners is generally a good indication of how much they have been loved.

Alligator Clutch, late 20th century, 9" x 7" .... **$200-$400**

Leslie Hindman Auctioneers

Alligator Clutch, late 20th century, 10" x 6" .... **$200-$400**

Leslie Hindman Auctioneers

Alligator Clutch, late 20th century, 8 1/2" x 5 1/2"............ **$200-$400**

Leslie Hindman Auctioneers

Alligator Clutch, late 20th century, 11 1/2" x 6"............... **$700-$900**

Leslie Hindman Auctioneers

Ann Turk, Crocodile, late 20th century, 11 1/2" x 10" .... **$100-$200**

Leslie Hindman Auctioneers

Apple, Snakeskin, mid-20th century, 9" x 7" .... **$100-$200**

Leslie Hindman Auctioneers

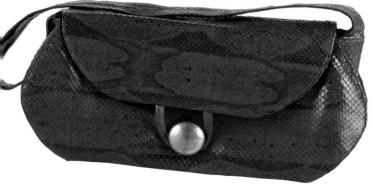

Snakeskin, mid-20th century, 11" x 5".............................. **$100-$200**

Leslie Hindman Auctioneers

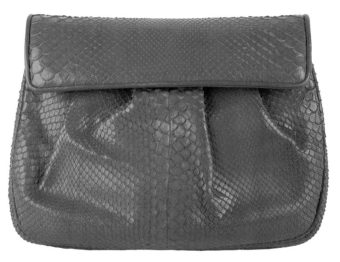

Bottega Veneta, Snakeskin, late 20th century, 9" x 7" .... **$200-$400**

Leslie Hindman Auctioneers

Carlos Falchi, Patchwork Skin, late 20th century, 12" x 6" .. **$100-$200**

Leslie Hindman Auctioneers

Carlos Falchi, Snakeskin, late 20th century, 9" x 5 1/2" .... **$100-$200**

Leslie Hindman Auctioneers

Carlos Falchi, Snakeskin, late 20th century, 11" x 20"....... **$100-$200**

Leslie Hindman Auctioneers

CeCe Cord, Lizard, late 20th century, 9" x 5" .... **$400-$600**

Leslie Hindman Auctioneers

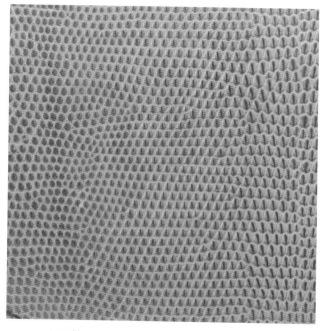

Lizard has extremely small scales giving a pebbled effect.

Chanel, Alligator, late 20th century, 11" x 8" .... **$1,000-$2,000**

Leslie Hindman Auctioneers

Chanel, Lizard, late 20th century, 7" x 5"............................ **$600-$800**

Leslie Hindman Auctioneers

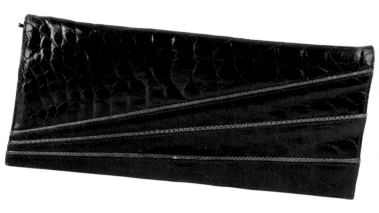

Charles Jourdan, Alligator, late 20th century, 11 1/2" x 5" .. **$100-$200**

Leslie Hindman Auctioneers

Crocodile Clutch, late 20th century, 9" x 6 1/2" .... **$100-$200**

Leslie Hindman Auctioneers

Crocodile Purse, mid-20th century, 7" x 6" .... **$400-$600**

Leslie Hindman Auctioneers

Crocodile Tote, late 20th century, 14" x 13"......................... **$400-$600**

Leslie Hindman Auctioneers

Dior, Alligator, late 20th century, 13" x 9" .... **$600-$800**

Leslie Hindman Auctioneers

Eel Skin Purse, late 20th century, 16" x 12".......................... **$100-$200**

Leslie Hindman Auctioneers

Fendi, Pony Hair, Mama Bag, late 20th century, 7 1/2" x 10".... **$400-$600**

Leslie Hindman Auctioneers

Finesse La Model, Lizard, late 20th century, 8" x 5 1/2".... **$300-$500**

Leslie Hindman Auctioneers

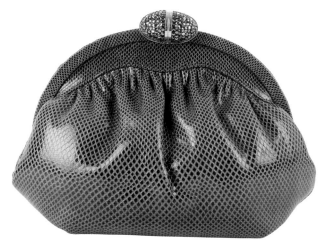

Finesse La Model, Lizard, late 20th century, 8" x 6" .... **$300-$500**

Leslie Hindman Auctioneers

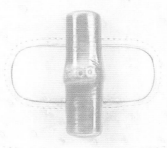

Gucci

Founded by Guccio Gucci as a leather goods company in 1921, Gucci's first notable success was in equestrian supplies. Upon gaining recognition, they used their equestrian roots to inspire much of the classic details we see today. The use of the stirrup and bit as well as the ribbon inspired by the saddle's girth can be seen in almost all of their handbag creations past and present. Another iconic attribute to Gucci's handbag is the use of bamboo, which began during WWII as a less expensive alternative. It is still used today.

Gucci, Lizard, late 20th century, 11 1/2" x 10"................**$800-$1,200**

Leslie Hindman Auctioneers

Gucci, Lizard, Clutch, late 20th century, 8" x 5" .... **$300-$500**

Leslie Hindman Auctioneers

Gucci, Ostrich, mid-20th century, 10 1/2" x 7" .... **$300-$500**

Leslie Hindman Auctioneers

Gucci, Ostrich, mid-20th century, 7" x 9 1/2" .... **$800-$1,200**

Leslie Hindman Auctioneers

Ostrich is one of the toughest and stiffest animal skins, and is easy to identify. It has small, evenly arranged bumps, known as quill follicles, which held the feathers.

Hermes

Hermes was founded in the early 19th century as a saddlery company and it was not until the introduction of more innovative transportation that they broadened their outreach to other forms of travel accessories. Their creations have always exuded impeccable craftsmanship. The most famous creations are the Kelly and Birkin bags. Made famous in the 1950s when Grace Kelly hid her rumored baby bump with it, the Kelly bag is the most recognizable in any handbag collection. Similarly, the Birkin was created when English singer/actress Jane Birkin told the CEO of Hermes in 1984 that she wanted the perfect weekend bag, describing in detail what it should include. The Birkin bag was based on the Haut à Courroies bag and is now the most coveted. Both bags have long waiting lists and are difficult to obtain, creating a strong secondary market.

These bags top the list for counterfeits. There are a few ways to tell if a bag is authentic. First and foremost, every Hermes bag created from 1971 going forward has a blind stamp somewhere on it. More specifically, the stamp on Kellys and Birkins is found on the underside of the right strap at the clasp and is a letter with a circle or square around it. (Started with A in 1971 the circle series runs through Z in 1996 and the square series started in 1997 moving in order to present day.) Another thing to keep in mind is that each of these bags is hand sewn. if the stitches look machine sewn, especially on the interior where the strap attaches to the back, then it is probably fake. Make sure that the key and lock have matching numbers and that all of the trademarks are in the correct spots.

Hermes, Berlingot, Ostrich, late 20th century,
  9 1/4" x 4 1/2" ....**$1,000-$2,000**

Leslie Hindman Auctioneers

Hermes, Birkin, Crocodile, late 20th century, 12" x 8 1/4"..**$15,000-$25,000**

Leslie Hindman Auctioneers

Hermes, Birkin, Crocodile, late 20th century,
12" x 8 1/4"..**$15,000-$25,000**

Leslie Hindman Auctioneers

Hermes, Birkin, Crocodile, late 20th century,
12" x 8 1/4"..**$15,000-$25,000**

Leslie Hindman Auctioneers

Niloticus Crocodile is the less expensive Hermes crocodile that has larger scales. There will always be this symbol if it is a Niloticus Crocodile bag.

Hermes, Birkin, Lizard, late 20th century, 10" x 8" ...**$10,000-$15,000**

Leslie Hindman Auctioneers

Hermes, Bolide, Ostrich, late 20th century,
10 1/2" x 7 1/2" ....**$3,000-$5,000**

Leslie Hindman Auctioneers

Hermes, Birkin, Ostrich, late 20th century, 12" x 9".......**$10,000-$15,000**

Leslie Hindman Auctioneers

Hermes, Constance, Lizard, late 20th century, 9" x 7" ..... **$1,500-$2,000**

Leslie Hindman Auctioneers

Hermes, Constance, Crocodile, late 20th century, 9" x 7".... **$3,000-$5,000**

Leslie Hindman Auctioneers

Hermes, Crocodile, late 20th century, 10" x 7" ....**$1,000-$2,000**

Leslie Hindman Auctioneers

Crocodile can look extremely similar to alligator and the easiest way to tell the difference is within a single scale. Crocodile will always have a pockmark near the edge of the scale that is not present in alligator.

Hermes, Kelly, Crocodile, late 20th century,
   10" x 7 1/2"..**$10,000-$15,000**

Leslie Hindman Auctioneers

Hermes, Kelly, Crocodile, mid-20th century,
14" x 10 1/2" .... **$10,000-$15,000**

Leslie Hindman Auctioneers

Hermes, Kelly, Crocodile, late 20th century, 12 1/2" x 10".................................**$10,000-$15,000**

Leslie Hindman Auctioneers

Porosus Crocodile is the most expensive hide Hermes has to offer. There will always be a symbol near the trademark if it is an exotic skin, and this one is specifically for Porosus Crocodile.

Gianfranco Ferre, Alligator, late 20th century, 9" x 5" .... **$500-$700**

Leslie Hindman Auctioneers

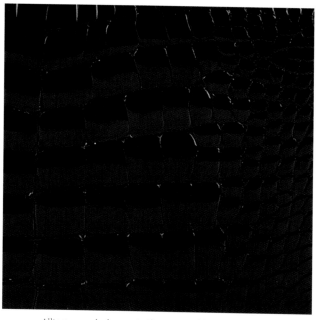

Alligator can look very similar to crocodile, but always has squarer scales with no pockmarks present. The size of each scale depends on the size or age or the alligator. Baby alligator is the most luxurious and supple, and has very small scales.

Jacomo, Alligator, mid-20th century, 7" x 5 1/2"............. **$800-$1,200**

Leslie Hindman Auctioneers

Jacomo, Alligator, mid-20th century, 8" x 5 1/2"............. **$800-$1,200**

Leslie Hindman Auctioneers

Jacomo, Lizard, mid-20th century, 9" x 5" .... **$200-$400**

Leslie Hindman Auctioneers

Jacomo, Snakeskin, late 20th century, 10" x 7" .... **$300-$500**

Leslie Hindman Auctioneers

Jacomo, Snakeskin, late 20th century, 9" x 6" .... **$400-$600**

Leslie Hindman Auctioneers

Judith Leiber, Alligator, late 20th century, 6 1/2" x 4" .... **$400-$600**

Leslie Hindman Auctioneers

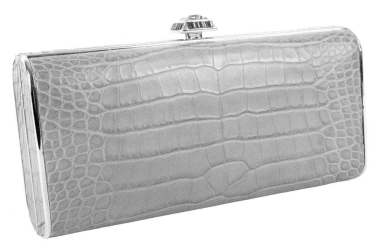

Judith Leiber, Alligator, late 20th century, 7" x 3 1/2" .... **$500-$700**

Leslie Hindman Auctioneers

Judith Leiber, Alligator, late 20th century, 9 1/2" x 5 1/2"... **$1,000-$2,000**

Leslie Hindman Auctioneers

Judith Leiber, Alligator, late 20th century, 14" x 9" ......**$1,000-$2,000**

Leslie Hindman Auctioneers

Judith Leiber, Lizard, late 20th century, 9" x 7".................. **$200-$400**

Leslie Hindman Auctioneers

Judith Leiber, Lizard, late 20th century, 11" x 8 1/2" .... **$200-$400**

Leslie Hindman Auctioneers

Judith Leiber, Lizard, late 20th century, 10" x 8" .... **$200-$400**

Leslie Hindman Auctioneers

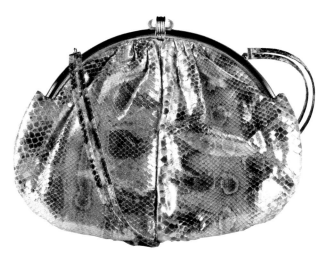

Judith Leiber, Python, late 20th century, 12" x 10 1/2" ...... **$300-$500**

Leslie Hindman Auctioneers

Judith Leiber, Lizard, late 20th century, 7 1/2" x 5 1/2" ..... **$500-$700**

Leslie Hindman Auctioneers

Judith Leiber, Snakeskin, late 20th century, 7" x 4" .... **$200-$400**

Leslie Hindman Auctioneers

Judith Leiber, Snakeskin, late 20th century, 9" x 6 1/2" ..... **$300-$500**

Leslie Hindman Auctioneers

Judith Leiber, Snakeskin, late 20th century, 15" x 8" ... **$1,000-$2,000**

Leslie Hindman Auctioneers

Kieselstein-Cord, Snakeskin, late 20th century, 8 3/4" x 5".. **$400-$600**

Leslie Hindman Auctioneers

Kieselstein-Cord, Python, late 20th century, 9 1/2" x 8" .... **$500-$700**

Leslie Hindman Auctioneers

Snakeskin is generally easy to spot because of its regular pattern. It is not extremely tough and may have lifting scales requiring a varnish coating.

Lana Marks, Crocodile, late 20th century, 12" x 6" ......**$1,500-$2,500**

Leslie Hindman Auctioneers

Leopard fur, mid-20th century, 7" x 12" .... **$200-$250**

Courtesy Stacy LoAlbo

Lucille de Paris, Alligator, mid-20th century, 9" x 9 1/2"... **$300-$500**

Leslie Hindman Auctioneers

Lucille de Paris, Alligator, mid-20th century, 10 1/2" x 8". **$300-$500**

Leslie Hindman Auctioneers

Mark Cross, Ostrich, mid-20th century, 10" x 7 1/2" .... **$100-$200**

Leslie Hindman Auctioneers

Meyers, Alligator, mid-20th century, 7" x 5" .... **$400-$600**

Leslie Hindman Auctioneers

Nancy Gonzalez, Crocodile, late 20th century, 8" x 7"....... **$400-$600**

Leslie Hindman Auctioneers

Nettie Rosenstein, Alligator, mid-20th century, 9" x 7"...... **$300-$500**

Leslie Hindman Auctioneers

Nettie Rosenstein, Leopard Fur, mid-20th century,
14 1/2" x 11"... **$800-$1,200**

Leslie Hindman Auctioneers

Nettie Rosenstein, Ostrich, mid-20th century, 9 1/2" x 7". **$100-$200**

Leslie Hindman Auctioneers

Nettie Rosenstein, Ostrich, mid-20th century, 9" x 4" .... **$100-$200**

Leslie Hindman Auctioneers

Ostrich, late 20th century, 9 1/2" x 8".............................. **$300-$500**

Leslie Hindman Auctioneers

Ostrich Clutch, late 20th century, 12" x 6 1/2" .... **$400-$600**

Leslie Hindman Auctioneers

Ostrich Clutch, late 20th century, 8" x 4 1/2"................... **$400-$600**

Leslie Hindman Auctioneers

Pony Hair, late 20th century, 10" x 8 1/2" .... **$50-$100**

Leslie Hindman Auctioneers

Prada, Pony Hair, late 20th century, 6" x 10".................... **$200-$400**

Leslie Hindman Auctioneers

Snakeskin, late 20th century, 6 1/2" x 5"............................ **$400-$600**

Leslie Hindman Auctioneers

Turtle, mid-20th century, 8 1/2" x 6" .... **$100-$200**

Leslie Hindman Auctioneers

Turtle can be mistaken for alligator. The easiest way to tell is by the shape of the scales. They are not as squared as alligator, but rather hexagonal or pentagonal, and the scales' sizing is not as even as alligator.

Versace, Alligator, late 20th century, 14" x 12"................... **$700-$900**

Leslie Hindman Auctioneers

Warman's Handbags Field Guide

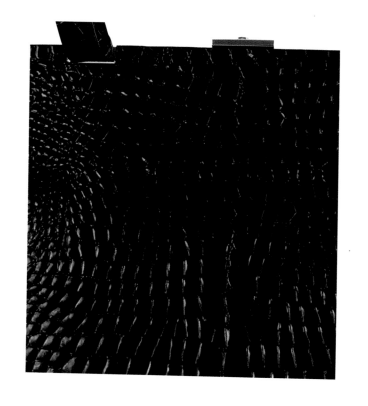

Iconic

The companies behind these handbags mostly got their start in travel and equestrian goods, and naturally progressed into creating handbags. These handbags are usually the easiest to recognize on someone's arm, generally intertwining the maker's logo into the designs, like Gucci and Louis Vuitton.

Condition Issues: Beware of counterfeits.

Bottega Veneta, late 20th century, 9 1/2" x 9" .... **$100-$200**

*Using only the finest Italian leather, Bottega Veneta is
known for their classic yet durable woven creations.*

Leslie Hindman Auctioneers

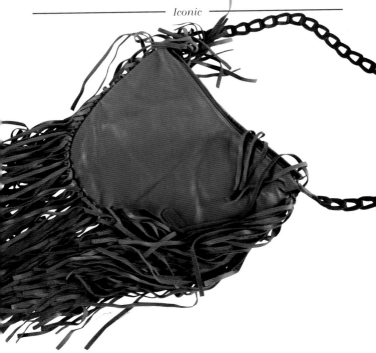

Carlos Falchi, late 20th century, 16" x 12" .... **$100-$200**

Famous for his fringe and cinched leather accessories,
Carlos Falchi bags are quintessential '80s.

Leslie Hindman Auctioneers

Carlos Falchi, mid-20th century, 13" x 11"........................ **$200-$400**

Leslie Hindman Auctioneers

Dior, contemporary, 9" x 6" .... **$200-$400**

Leslie Hindman Auctioneers

Dior, contemporary, 12" x 6" .... **$200-$400**

Leslie Hindman Auctioneers

Dior, late 20th century, 11" x 7" .... **$50-$100**

Leslie Hindman Auctioneers

Fendi, Baguette, contemporary, 10" x 6".............................. **$100-$200**

Leslie Hindman Auctioneers

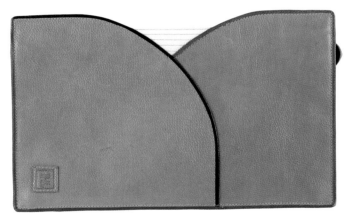

Fendi, late 20th century, 13" x 8".. **$100-$200**

Leslie Hindman Auctioneers

Fendi, late 20th century, 12" x 9" .... **$100-$200**

Leslie Hindman Auctioneers

Fendi, Mama Bag, contemporary, 12" x 9".......................... **$100-$200**

Leslie Hindman Auctioneers

Ferragamo, contemporary, 9" x 6 1/2".............................. **$100-$200**

Leslie Hindman Auctioneers

Ferragamo, contemporary, 11 1/2" x 8 1/2".........................**$200-$400**

Leslie Hindman Auctioneers

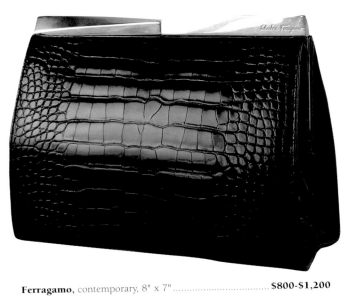

Ferragamo, contemporary, 8" x 7" .... **$800-$1,200**

Leslie Hindman Auctioneers

Ferragamo, late 20th century, 14" x 10" .... **$50-$100**

Leslie Hindman Auctioneers

Gucci, contemporary, 11" x 5".. **$200-$400**

Leslie Hindman Auctioneers

Gucci, contemporary, 12 1/2" x 9" .... **$200-$400**

With multiple variations over the years, this handbag became known as the "Jackie O" because of her penchant for the Gucci creation.

Leslie Hindman Auctioneers

Gucci, contemporary, 10 1/2" x 7" .... **$200-$400**

Leslie Hindman Auctioneers

Gucci, contemporary, 10" x 8".. **$300-$500**

Leslie Hindman Auctioneers

Gucci, contemporary, 13" x 9 1/2" .... **$300-$500**

Leslie Hindman Auctioneers

Gucci, contemporary, 12" x 6".. **$300-$500**

Leslie Hindman Auctioneers

Gucci, late 20th century, 8" x 7".. **$100-$200**

Leslie Hindman Auctioneers

Gucci, Double-Sided Box Bag, mid-20th century, 8" x 5" .... **$300-$500**

Leslie Hindman Auctioneers

Gucci, Double-Sided Box Bag, mid-20th century, 8" x 5".... **$300-$500**

Leslie Hindman Auctioneers

Gucci, late 20th century, 10" x 9"...**$200-$400**

Leslie Hindman Auctioneers

Gucci, late 20th century, 17" x 14".................................... **$200-$400**

Leslie Hindman Auctioneers

Gucci, late 20th century, 15" x 12"...................................... **$200-$400**

Leslie Hindman Auctioneers

Gucci, late 20th century, 15" x 11".................................... **$100-$200**

Leslie Hindman Auctioneers

Gucci, late 20th century, 11" X 7" .... **$200-$400**

Leslie Hindman Auctioneers

Gucci, late 20th century, 11 1/2" x 8" .... **$200-$400**

Leslie Hindman Auctioneers

Gucci, late 20th century, 12" x 12"..................................... **$200-$400**

Leslie Hindman Auctioneers

Gucci, late 20th century, 15" x 11"...................................... **$300-$500**

Leslie Hindman Auctioneers

Gucci, mid-20th century, 10" x 7".. **$200-$400**

Leslie Hindman Auctioneers

Gucci, Water Bottle Tote, contemporary, 9" x 3 1/2" .... **$100-$200**

Leslie Hindman Auctioneers

Jean Paul Gaultier, late 20th century, 11" x 10" .... **$150-$250**

Leslie Hindman Auctioneers

Louis Vuitton

In the mid-19th century, Louis Vuitton founded his company as a "malletier," creating trunks for Paris' elite society. With its recognizable monogram and Damier canvas (used for authenticity purposes at the turn of the century), these details are widely used in their designs today. In the late 1950s, the company started creating handbags and small leather accessories. Some of the most recognizable creations today are the Pouchette and the Speedy bag.

The market for counterfeiting handbags probably got its start with Louis Vuitton; they seem to be on every street corner in every big city. An easy telltale sign is in the leather handle, which when new has a pink tinge, but always wears into brown with use. If there is a worn handbag with a pink-hued handle, then it is most likely fake. The most widely knocked-off medium for Louis Vuitton is the monogram canvas, which should feel like a thick, coated material that is extremely durable. Look for all of the necessary trademarks, as well.

Louis Vuitton, contemporary, 13" x 10" .... **$700-$900**

Leslie Hindman Auctioneers

Louis Vuitton, contemporary, with matching wallet,
11 1/2" x 10"... **$800-$1,200**

Leslie Hindman Auctioneers

Louis Vuitton, Damier canvas, late 20th century, 10" x 8"... **$200-$400**

Leslie Hindman Auctioneers

Louis Vuitton, Damier canvas, late 20th century, 9" x 8" ... **$400-$600**

Leslie Hindman Auctioneers

Louis Vuitton's distinctive Damier canvas has a checkerboard pattern and is trimmed with leather.

Louis Vuitton, late 20th century, 11" x 9" .... **$200-$400**

Leslie Hindman Auctioneers

Louis Vuitton, late 20th century, 16" x 12" .... **$400-$600**

Leslie Hindman Auctioneers

Louis Vuitton, late 20th century, 14" x 8" .... **$400-$600**

Leslie Hindman Auctioneers

Louis Vuitton, late 20th century, 12" x 9" .... **$700-$900**

Leslie Hindman Auctioneers

Louis Vuitton, late 20th century, 11" x 6" .... **$800-$1,200**

Leslie Hindman Auctioneers

Louis Vuitton, monogram denim, late 20th century, 12" x 9" ..**$400-$600**

Leslie Hindman Auctioneers

Louis Vuitton, Pouchette, late 20th century, 9" x 5"............ **$200-$400**

Leslie Hindman Auctioneers

Louis Vuitton, Saddle Bag, late 20th century, 12" x 9" .... **$400-$600**

Leslie Hindman Auctioneers

Paloma Picasso, late 20th century, 8" x 8".........................**$100-$200**

Leslie Hindman Auctioneers

Prada, contemporary, 14 1/2" x 10 1/2".............................. **$100-$200**

Leslie Hindman Auctioneers

Prada, contemporary, 12" x 7" .... **$100-$200**

Leslie Hindman Auctioneers

Prada, contemporary, 11" x 7" .... **$200-$400**

Leslie Hindman Auctioneers

Prada, nylon, contemporary, 10" x 4" .... **$100-$200**

Leslie Hindman Auctioneers

Prada, nylon, contemporary, 9 1/4" x 4 1/2" .... **$100-$200**

Leslie Hindman Auctioneers

Prada, nylon, contemporary, 11" x 7" .... **$100-$200**

Leslie Hindman Auctioneers

Yves Saint Laurent, late 20th century, 8" x 6".................... **$100-$200**

Ritchies Auctioneers

Yves Saint Laurent, late 20th century, 10" x 7" .... **$200-$400**

Leslie Hindman Auctioneers

Yves Saint Laurent, late 20th century, 10" x 7 1/2" .... **$200-$400**

Leslie Hindman Auctioneers

Pop Art/Novelty

Whether it is a Dallas telephone bag that can be plugged in for use or a contemporary artist giving his impression on a tote, these bags are generally highly collectable because of their uniqueness and artistic quality. Most have been inspired by pop culture to fulfill an artistic and humorous role.

Chanel, Water Bottle Bag, late 20th century, 12" x 8 1/2" ... **$600-$800**

Leslie Hindman Auctioneers

Claudio Merazzi, Fish, late 20th century, 10 1/4" x 5 1/2" **$400-$600**

Leslie Hindman Auctioneers

Dallas, Telephone Bag, late 20th century, 13 1/2" x 11"...... **$300-$500**

Leslie Hindman Auctioneers

With a cord to plug into the wall wherever you might need to phone someone, this bag was humorous as well as functional during its heyday.

Enid Collins, Love Box Bag, mid-20th century,
8 1/2" x 5 1/2" x 4" .... **$200-$400**

Leslie Hindman Auctioneers

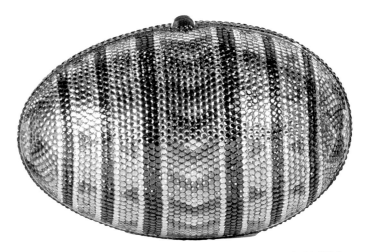

Finesse la Model, Egg Minaudiere, late 20th century, 6" x 4" ..**$100-$200**

Leslie Hindman Auctioneers

Finesse la Model, Owl Minaudiere, late 20th century,
5 1/2" x 4"... **$100-$200**

Leslie Hindman Auctioneers

Flamingo Purse, Lucite, Leather, mid-20th century, 11" x 10" .... **$200-$400**

Leslie Hindman Auctioneers

Isabel Canovas, late 20th century, 8" x 8" .... **$200-$400**

Leslie Hindman Auctioneers

Jamin Puech, late 20th century, 7" x 5" .... **$50-$100**

Leslie Hindman Auctioneers

Judith Leiber, Egg Minaudiere, late 20th century,
6" x 4"...**$1,000-$2,000**

Leslie Hindman Auctioneers

Judith Leiber, Horse Minaudiere, late 20th century, 6" x 4" .... **$1,000-$2,000**

Leslie Hindman Auctioneers

Judith Leiber, Humpty Dumpty Minaudiere, late 20th century,
5" x 4"...**$1,000-$2,000**

Leslie Hindman Auctioneers

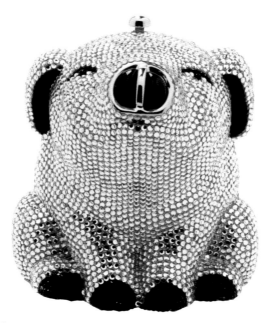

Judith Leiber, Pig Minaudiere, late 20th century, 4" x 4"... **$1,000-$2,000**

Leslie Hindman Auctioneers

Judith Leiber, Quail Minaudiere, late 20th century,
5" x 5" .... **$1,000-$2,000**

Leslie Hindman Auctioneers

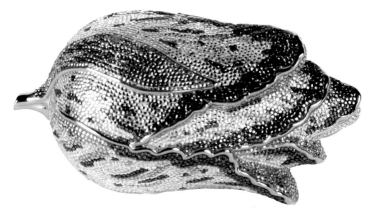

Judith Leiber, Tulip Minaudiere, late 20th century,
6" x 3 1/2"..**$1,000-$2,000**

Leslie Hindman Auctioneers

Koret, Opera Bag, with binoculars, mid-20th century,
6 1/2" x 4" .... **$800-$1,200**

Leslie Hindman Auctioneers

Louis Vuitton, Cherry Cerises, contemporary, 14" x 15" .... **$600-$800**

Leslie Hindman Auctioneers

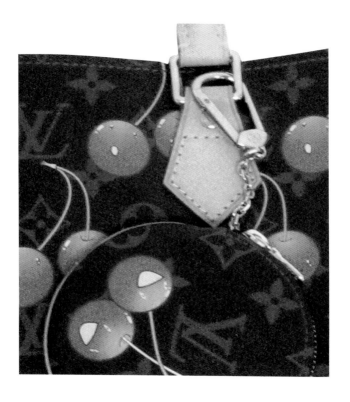

Louis Vuitton Commissioned Artists

In the late 1990s, Louis Vuitton became a full-service fashion house offering prêt a porter fashion, and selected Marc Jacobs to be at the helm. Jacobs commissioned renowned artist Takashi Murakami and fashion designer Stephen Sprouse to create their versions of classic Louis Vuitton handbags. In 2001, the Graffiti bag was introduced by Sprouse and sold out almost immediately. In 2003, Murakami's designs were released, ranging from the monogram canvas in a multicolor print to the more collectible Smiley Face cherry blossoms atop the classic monogram canvas.

Murakami for Louis Vuitton, contemporary, 9" x 5" .... **$300-$500**

Leslie Hindman Auctioneers

Murakami for Louis Vuitton,
contemporary, 11" x 5".............**$600-$800**

Leslie Hindman Auctioneers

Stephen Sprouse for Louis Vuitton, Graffiti Bag, contemporary,
10" x 7 1/2"...$1,500-$2,500

Wright

Magazine Clutch, late 20th century, 12" x 4 3/4"................ **$50-$100**

Leslie Hindman Auctioneers

Midas, Elephant, mid-20th century, 13" x 13" .... **$400-$600**

Leslie Hindman Auctioneers

Midas, Poodle, mid-20th century, 10" x 8" .... **$150-$250**

Leslie Hindman Auctioneers

Midas, Road Runner, mid-20th century, 13" x 10" .... **$50-$100**

Leslie Hindman Auctioneers

Midas, Wheat, mid-20th century, 11" x 9" .... **$50-$100**

Leslie Hindman Auctioneers

Moschino

Franco Moschino will always be remembered for his rebellious nature in fashion, always placing humor within his designs. Well known for his phrase,"Stop the Fashion System," this resonates well with his handbag designs. The best examples of this are his rendition of the Hermes Bolide bag covered with dripping chocolate, or his evening bag in the shape of a tuxedo. Moschino's designs are always playful and never boring.

Moschino, Fudge the Fashionista, Let Them Eat Cake, late 20th century, 14" x 11"..**$800-$1,200**

One of his most recognizable creations, Moschino poked fun at the Hermes Bolide-carrying woman with this dripping manifesto.

Leslie Hindman Auctioneers

Moschino, Hip Bag, late 20th century, 10" x 4" .... **$50-$100**

Leslie Hindman Auctioneers

Moschino, late 20th century, 10" x 6" .... **$100-$200**

Leslie Hindman Auctioneers

Moschino, Dice, late 20th century, 7" x 7" x 8" .... **$100-$200**

Leslie Hindman Auctioneers

Moschino, Forever … Kelly, late 20th century, 12" x 10"….. **$100-$200**

Leslie Hindman Auctioneers

Moschino, late 20th century, 8" x 7" .... **$100-$200**

Leslie Hindman Auctioneers

Moschino, Loose Keys, late 20th century, 12" x 9" .... **$100-$200**

Leslie Hindman Auctioneers

Moschino, Smiley Face, late 20th century, 13" x 12" .... **$100-$200**

Leslie Hindman Auctioneers

Moschino, Teddy Bear, late 20th century, 17" x 10" .... **$100-$200**

Leslie Hindman Auctioneers

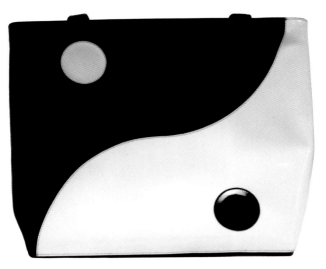

Moschino, Yin Yang, late 20th century, 13" x 12" .... **$100-$200**

Leslie Hindman Auctioneers

Moschino, late 20th century, 12" x 10" .... **$200-$400**

Leslie Hindman Auctioneers

Moschino, Tuxedo, late 20th century, 10" x 9 1/2" .... **$300-$500**

Leslie Hindman Auctioneers

Moschino, late 20th century, 14" x 11" .... **$300-$500**

Leslie Hindman Auctioneers

Moschino, late 20th century, 12" x 9" .... **$300-$500**

Leslie Hindman Auctioneers

Moschino, late 20th century, 14" x 10 1/2"........................ **$300-$500**

Leslie Hindman Auctioneers

Moschino, Watermelon, late 20th century, 10" x 5 1/2" ...... **$400-$600**

Leslie Hindman Auctioneers

Moschino, late 20th century, 8 1/2" x 8" .... **$400-$600**

Leslie Hindman Auctioneers

Moschino, Lip Locked, late 20th century, 8 1/2" x 8" .... **$100-$200**

Leslie Hindman Auctioneers

Moschino, Olive Oyl, late 20th century, 13 3/4" x 14 1/2".....**$800-$1,200**

Leslie Hindman Auctioneers

Plastic Football Purse, mid-20th century, 12" x 7" .... **$200-$400**

Leslie Hindman Auctioneers

Saks Fifth Avenue, Penny-Wise, Pound-Foolish, mid-20th century,
13 1/2" x 11 1/2" .... **$100-$200**

Leslie Hindman Auctioneers

Surrealistic Leather Purse, late 20th century, 11" x 9" ..... **$100-$200**

Leslie Hindman Auctioneers

Surrealistic Leather Purse, late 20th century, 11" x 9" ..... **$100-$200**

Leslie Hindman Auctioneers

Woven Cigarette Pack Purse, mid-century, 5" x 8"............ **$125-$175**

Courtesy Stacy LoAlbo

Timeless

Always deemed classic in today's world, these handbags were the pinnacle of change over the past century. From Coco Chanel adding a simple shoulder strap to the average handbag, or the upholstery-like Roberta di Camerino bags, these classics have shaped and inspired the rest.

Condition Issues: Beware of counterfeits.

Cartier, late 20th century, 12" x 10".................................... **$200-$400**

Leslie Hindman Auctioneers

Cartier, late 20th century, 10" x 9".. **$200-$400**

Leslie Hindman Auctioneers

Chanel

A true innovator in woman's fashion, Coco Chanel's creations changed the shape of handbags. Her inspiration was a soldier's shoulder bag and her purpose was to free women from the hand-held bag common in the '50s. The result was the "2.55" named for the date it debuted, February 1955. What started as a classic, diagonally quilted shoulder bag has been reinvented over the past 50 years to make it Chanel's most recognizable and collected piece.

Chanel bags are also widely knocked off. When examining a bag made of leather, make sure that the material is extremely high quality. The CC logo should be sewn precisely and there are generally no flaws around this area of the bag. Another red flag is the chain shoulder strap, which is always dipped in gold or other precious metals and has a substantial weight to it. If there is strange wear to the strap or it seems to be a lightweight chain for the amount of metal used, it is most likely fake. In more recent bags there is also a hologram, generally on the interior corner, to help curb counterfeits.

Chanel, Backpack, late 20th century, 12" x 10".................... **$200-$400**

Leslie Hindman Auctioneers

Chanel, late 20th century, 14" x 13" .... **$500-$700**

Leslie Hindman Auctioneers

With opulence always in mind, this pebbled leather is called "caviar" by Chanel for its resemblance to the delicacy.

Chanel, contemporary, 10" x 6" .... **$500-$700**

Leslie Hindman Auctioneers

Chanel, Belt Bag, late 20th century, 6 1/2" x 6 1/2" .... **$200-$400**

Leslie Hindman Auctioneers

Chanel, Briefcase, late 20th century, 14 1/2" x 11"........**$1,000-$2,000**

Leslie Hindman Auctioneers

Chanel, Hip Bag, late 20th century, 10 1/2" x 6"................. **$600-$800**

Leslie Hindman Auctioneers

Chanel, late 20th century, 9" x 7" .... **$400-$600**

Leslie Hindman Auctioneers

Chanel, late 20th century, 9" x 6" .... **$400-$600**

Leslie Hindman Auctioneers

More contemporary Chanel handbags are clear inspirations of the "2.55" (the bag named for the day of its introduction, February 1955) and yet have their own characteristics, like swirled sewn leather, seen here, rather than the classic quilted style.

Chanel, late 20th century, 9" x 7" .... **$600-$800**

Leslie Hindman Auctioneers

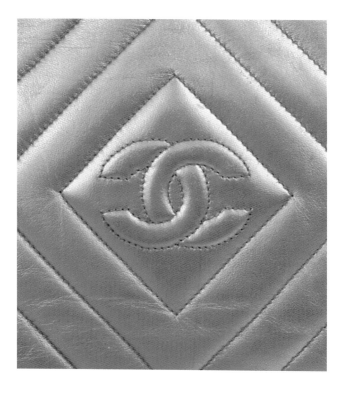

Chanel, late 20th century, 10" x 7" .... **$400-$600**

Leslie Hindman Auctioneers

Chanel, late 20th century, 9" x 5 1/2" .... **$400-$600**

Leslie Hindman Auctioneers

Chanel, late 20th century, 10" x 6" .... **$400-$600**

Leslie Hindman Auctioneers

Chanel, late 20th century, 7" x 5" .... **$200-$400**

Leslie Hindman Auctioneers

Chanel, late 20th century, 7 1/2" x 5" .... **$400-$600**

Leslie Hindman Auctioneers

Chanel, late 20th century, 9" x 7" .... **$600-$800**

Leslie Hindman Auctioneers

Chanel, late 20th century, 8" x 6" .... **$400-$600**

Leslie Hindman Auctioneers

Chanel, late 20th century, 5 1/2" x 4" .... **$400-$600**

Leslie Hindman Auctioneers

Chanel, late 20th century, 9" x 8" .... **$600-$800**

Leslie Hindman Auctioneers

Chanel, late 20th century, 13" x 9" .... **$800-$1,200**

Leslie Hindman Auctioneers

Chanel, late 20th century, 10" x 6" .... **$600-$800**

Leslie Hindman Auctioneers

Chanel, late 20th century, 7" x 6" .... **$400-$600**

Leslie Hindman Auctioneers

Chanel, late 20th century, 12" x 9" .... **$500-$700**

Leslie Hindman Auctioneers

Chanel, late 20th century, 15" x 9" .... **$600-$800**

Leslie Hindman Auctioneers

Chanel, late 20th century, 11 1/2" x 10" .... **$800-$1,200**

Leslie Hindman Auctioneers

Chanel, late 20th century, 12" x 10" .... **$800-$1,200**

Leslie Hindman Auctioneers

Chanel, 2.55 Bag, mid-20th century, 10" x 6" ....**$3,000-$5,000**

*Simply by lengthening a handle, woman everywhere
were freed from clutching a cumbersome bag.*

Leslie Hindman Auctioneers

Chanel, late 20th century, 12" x 11" .... **$600-$800**

Leslie Hindman Auctioneers

Chanel, late 20th century, 11" x 6" .... **$800-$1,200**

Leslie Hindman Auctioneers

Chanel, mid-20th century, 10" x 7" ....**$1,000-$2,000**

Leslie Hindman Auctioneers

Chanel, late 20th century, 19" x 12" .... **$600-$800**

Leslie Hindman Auctioneers

Chanel, late 20th century, 13" x 9" .... **$600-$800**

Leslie Hindman Auctioneers

Chanel, late 20th century, 7 3/4" x 5" .... **$200-$400**

Leslie Hindman Auctioneers

Goyard, contemporary, 16" x 12".................................$800-$1,200

Leslie Hindman Auctioneers

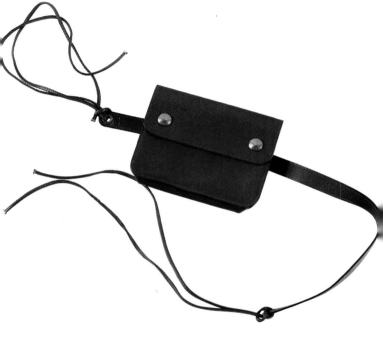

Hermes, Belt Bag, late 20th century, 5 1/2" x 4" .... **$100-$200**

Leslie Hindman Auctioneers

Hermes, Clutch, mid-20th century, 9 1/2" x 6" .... **$500-$700**

Leslie Hindman Auctioneers

Hermes, Birkin, contemporary, 12" x 8".......................**$5,000-$7,000**

Leslie Hindman Auctioneers

Hermes, Birkin, contemporary, 12 1/2" x 10"................ **$7,000-$9,000**

Leslie Hindman Auctioneers

Hermes, Birkin, contemporary, 10" x 7 1/2".................**$7,000-$9,000**

Leslie Hindman Auctioneers

Hermes, Birkin, contemporary, 12" x 8" ....**$7,000-$9,000**

Leslie Hindman Auctioneers

Hermes, Birkin, contemporary, 14" x 9 1/2"..................**$7,000-$9,000**

Leslie Hindman Auctioneers

Hermes, Shoulder Birkin, contemporary, 16 1/2" x 7" .. **$6,000-$8,000**

Leslie Hindman Auctioneers

Hermes, Constance, canvas, late 20th century, 9" x 7" .... **$500-$700**

Leslie Hindman Auctioneers

Hermes, Constance, late 20th century, 8 1/2" x 7" .... **$1,000-$2,000**

Leslie Hindman Auctioneers

Hermes, mid-20th century, 9 1/2" x 6" .... **$300-$500**

Leslie Hindman Auctioneers

Hermes, Dalvy, contemporary, 12" x 10" .... **$700-$900**

Leslie Hindman Auctioneers

Hermes, Envelope Clutch, contemporary, 11 3/4" x 8" .... **$500-$700**

Leslie Hindman Auctioneers

Hermes, Envelope Clutch, contemporary, 11 1/2" x 7 1/2". **$500-$700**

Leslie Hindman Auctioneers

Hermes, Haut a Courroies, contemporary, 12 1/2" x 10" . **$6,000-$8,000**

Leslie Hindman Auctioneers

Hermes, Herbag, contemporary, 18" x 15 3/4" (larger) .... **$800-$1,200**

A more utilitarian approach for Hermes, the Herbag is interchangeable to fit both small and large contents with one purchase.

Leslie Hindman Auctioneers

Hermes, Kelly, late 20th century, 12 1/2" x 9" .... **$3,000-$5,000**

Leslie Hindman Auctioneers

Hermes, Kelly, contemporary, 14" x 10 1/4" ....**$3,000-$5,000**

Leslie Hindman Auctioneers

Hermes, Kelly, contemporary, 12 1/2" x 9"....................**$5,000-$7,000**

Leslie Hindman Auctioneers

Hermes, Kelly, contemporary, 12 1/2" x 9" ....**$5,000-$7,000**

Leslie Hindman Auctioneers

Hermes, Kelly Lakis, contemporary, 16" x 10 1/2" ....**$3,000-$5,000**

There are multiple versions of the classic
Hermes Kelly, including this example, the Lakis.

Leslie Hindman Auctioneers

Hermes, Kelly, contemporary, 14" x 11" ....**$10,000-$15,000**

This is a limited-edition design by
Jean Paul Gaultier that is trimmed in shearing.

Leslie Hindman Auctioneers

Hermes, Kilt Bag, late 20th century, 13 1/2" x 12" ....**$1,000-$2,000**

Leslie Hindman Auctioneers

Hermes, Le Trim, late 20th century, 14" x 13 1/2" ....**$1,500-$2,500**

Leslie Hindman Auctioneers

Hermes, Le Trim, mid-20th century, 12" x 8 1/2" .... **$1,500-$2,500**

Made famous by Jackie Onassis, this a handbag classic.

Leslie Hindman Auctioneers

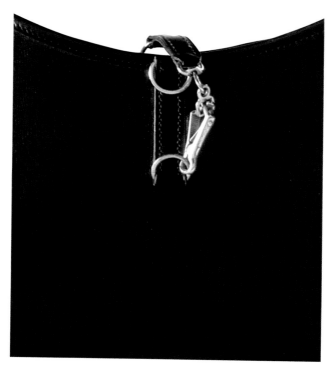

Hermes, Lindy, contemporary, 12" x 8" ....**$3,000-$5,000**

Leslie Hindman Auctioneers

Hermes, late 20th century, 12 1/2" x 9 1/2" ....**$1,500-$2,500**

Leslie Hindman Auctioneers

Hermes, Mini Kelly, late 20th century, 7 1/2" x 6".........**$2,000-$3,000**

Leslie Hindman Auctioneers

Hermes, Omnibus, contemporary, 10" x 9".................**$3,000-$5,000**

Leslie Hindman Auctioneers

Hermes, late 20th century, 12 1/2" x 10" ....**$1,000-$2,000**

Leslie Hindman Auctioneers

Hermes, Plume, late 20th century, 13" x 9".................$1,000-$2,000

Leslie Hindman Auctioneers

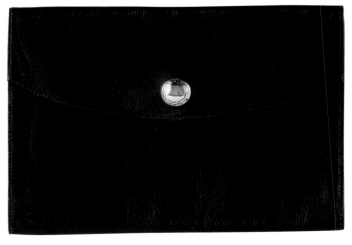

Hermes, Rio Clutch, contemporary, 9 1/2" x 7" .... **$500-$700**

Leslie Hindman Auctioneers

Hermes, mid-20th century, 11" x 7 1/2" .... **$300-$500**

Leslie Hindman Auctioneers

Hermes, late 20th century, 9 1/2" x 9 1/2" .... **$300-$500**

Leslie Hindman Auctioneers

Hermes, Vespa, late 20th century, 12" x 11"..................... **$800-$1,200**

Leslie Hindman Auctioneers

Hermes, late 20th century, 8" x 6" .... **$300-$500**

Leslie Hindman Auctioneers

Hermes, late 20th century, 11" x 9" .... **$300-$500**

Leslie Hindman Auctioneers

Hermes, late 20th century, 15" x 14" .... **$800-$1,200**

Leslie Hindman Auctioneers

Hermes, contemporary, 11 1/2" x 11" .... **$800-$1,200**

Leslie Hindman Auctioneers

Kieselstein-Cord, late 20th century, 12" x 9" .... **$200-$400**

Leslie Hindman Auctioneers

Kieselstein-Cord, late 20th century, 8 1/2" x 7" .... **$400-$600**

Leslie Hindman Auctioneers

Kieselstein-Cord, late 20th century, 8 1/2" x 7" .... **$600-$800**

Leslie Hindman Auctioneers

Kieselstein-Cord, late 20th century, 9" x 5 1/2" .... **$600-$800**

Leslie Hindman Auctioneers

Kieselstein-Cord, late 20th century, 7" x 7" .... **$200-$400**

Leslie Hindman Auctioneers

Kieselstein-Cord, late 20th century, 8 1/2" x 8" .... **$800-$1,200**

Leslie Hindman Auctioneers

Kieselstein-Cord, Suede, late 20th century, 8" x 7" .... **$600-$800**

Leslie Hindman Auctioneers

Kieselstein-Cord, Nylon, late 20th century, 12" x 9".......... **$200-$400**

Leslie Hindman Auctioneers

Roberta di Camerino

Known for her generally dark green, red and blue colors within cut-velvet designs, Giuliana Coen Camerino (born in Venice in 1920 and doing business under the name Roberta di Camerino) designed her first handbags while in neutral Switzerland during WWII. Those handbags became an instant success internationally with high society. After the war, she returned to Venice to continue her work. With the rich upholstery-like fabrics and durable brass, these bags were truly revolutionary. In 1956, she was awarded the Neiman Marcus award, and her creations are highly collectible today.

Roberta di Camerino, mid-20th century, 9 3/4" x 8 1/2" .. **$100-$200**

Leslie Hindman Auctioneers

Roberta di Camerino, mid-20th century, 9" x 8"............... **$300-$500**

Leslie Hindman Auctioneers

Roberta di Camerino, mid-20th century, 11" x 8"............. **$200-$400**

Leslie Hindman Auctioneers

Roberta di Camerino, mid-20th century, 10" x 8"............. **$200-$400**

Leslie Hindman Auctioneers

Roberta di Camerino, mid-20th century, 14" x 10" .... **$700-$900**

Leslie Hindman Auctioneers

Roberta di Camerino, mid-20th century, 11" x 9"............ **$300-$500**

Leslie Hindman Auctioneers

Roberta di Camerino, mid-20th century, 9" x 8".............. **$300-$500**

Leslie Hindman Auctioneers

Roberta di Camerino, mid-20th century, 9" x 6"............... **$300-$500**

Leslie Hindman Auctioneers

Roberta di Camerino, late 20th century, 15" x 10" .... **$300-$500**

Leslie Hindman Auctioneers

Roberta di Camerino, late 20th century, 10" x 7 1/2" .... **$300-$500**

Leslie Hindman Auctioneers

Resources

Auctions:

Leslie Hindman Auctioneers, Chicago; www.lesliehindman.com
Kerry Taylor Auctions, London; www.kerrytaylorauctions.com
Christie's South Kensington, London; www.christies.com
Karen Augusta Antique Lace & Fashion; www.antique-fashion.com
Caroline Ashleigh Associates LLC; www.auctionyourart.com

Vintage Shows:

Manhattan Vintage Clothing Show, NYC; www.manhattanvintage.com
Cats Pajamas Productions, IL, MN, MI; www.catspajamasproductions.net
Miami Vintage Clothing & Accessories Show; miamivintageclothingshow.com
Vintage Fashion Expo, CA; www.vintageexpo.com

Online:

www.vintageacademe.com
www.ebay.com
www.ladybaginternational.com
www.antiquedress.com
forum.purseblog.com
www.bagborroworsteal.com

Retail:

The Way We Wore, Los Angeles; www.thewaywewore.com
Decades, Los Angeles; www.decadesinc.com
Torso Vintages, San Francisco; www.torsovintages.com
Resurrection Vintage Clothing, New York; 212-625-1374

Index

Find the Value of Vintage

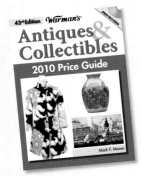